Beyond an ornate iron gate, spring's first flowers greet visitors.

Coreopsis blossom in front of this reconstructed log cabin in the Pioneer Museum complex.

Red-and-white quilts cheer the guest room of this converted rock barn dating from 1889.

Fredericksburg, Texas

Living with the Past

Text by
Don & Lynn Watt

Photography by
Michael Mehl

Shearer Publishing / Fredericksburg, Texas

© *Copyright* 1987 *by* Don Watt
Library of Congress Cataloging-in-Publication Data

Watt, Don, 1940–
Fredericksburg, Texas, living with the past.

1. Fredericksburg (Tex.)—Description—Views.
2. Architecture, Domestic—Texas—Fredericksburg—
Pictorial works.   3. Dwellings—Texas—Fredericksburg—
Pictorial works.   I. Watt, Lynn, 1939–   .   II. Title.
F394.F9W37   1987   976.4′65   87-20486
ISBN 0-940672-42-1

Dedicated to those pioneers, both
old and new, whose love of
the land and love of
their homes made
this book
possible.

A windmill casts its shadow on the tin roof of an old stone barn—now a bed-and-breakfast guest house.

THE PEDERNALES River flows through a fertile valley surrounded by chalky limestone hills in much the same way it has flowed for countless centuries, indifferent to time. It surges over its banks after thunderous spring rains only to become a lazy narrow stream in the aridness of August. Its deposits of sediment and soil accumulated over eons; its lush grasses fed and protected bear and wolves, deer and the nocturnal ringtail. Indian tribes migrated to and from the Pedernales, using the flint that lined the riverbed for tools and weapons and feeding off the game that roamed its banks.

In 1846 a brave group of German immigrants, 120 strong, made its way overland from the Texas Gulf Coast and settled in that valley which then was on the western frontier. Under the auspices of the Society for the Protection of German Immigrants in Texas, they named their new colony Fredericksburg. That first year the new settlers hurriedly erected temporary shelters that were little more than huts made of poles and grasses chinked with clay and moss. The first year they survived an epidemic of cholera and raids by hostile Comanches and began to cope with an unpredictable environment.

Today modern highways cut through the valley, bringing in visitors from around the world to walk Fredericksburg's historic main street.

This weathered wooden barn from the nineteenth century has been adapted to shelter cars of this century.

Norfolk sheep look curiously at the intrusion on their grazing.

The swept yard was the practical nineteenth-century gardener's answer to weeds and mowing. There are several of these charming old-time gardens in Fredericksburg.

They sit in the beer gardens, sample the pastries, and buy new "old" items and antiques from the shops. But they come not only to see and to buy but also to feel, to get a sense of place, to absorb the values that have disappeared from most of modern America.

The values are those that brought the first Germans to this valley, that enabled them to move from the first rudimentary huts into *fachwerk* cabins and then to erect the limestone houses with walls a foot and a half thick and lintel stones that weighed several hundred pounds. Those houses still dot the hillsides around the town and lie randomly scattered up and down the treelined streets.

The immigrants had a tenacity that caused them to put down

their roots and go no farther. But it was more than that, more than tenacity or pride. There was a sense of rightness, of deliberateness, a determination that they carried through their religion, whether Catholic or Protestant, and through their sense of family, which extended beyond cousins and uncles and included neighbors and friends who were willing to risk all that they had, even their very lives, to establish a free and independent way of life.

The limestone houses and barns reflect that sense of permanence, the determination not only to survive but also to persevere and remain a community. The houses are solid—they "stand on their own two feet" in a self-sufficient way—but are tied in a close network to each other through a shared style, through the common labor that was necessary in their construction, and through the stability that they exhibit as many of them enter the second century of their existence.

Beyond the shops, beyond the beer and the *wurst,* the tourists feel something more. They feel the sense of place, of permanence and deliberateness, of steadfastness to a vision of a better future. These are the intangible values that visitors come to Fredericksburg for, and when they leave, they hope to take some of that with them.

Others, attracted by those same qualities, have come and stayed. Those *auslanders* (outsiders) have continued in the spirit of the place by restoring and adapting the old homes and buildings for modern use while retaining the integrity of their style. This book samples some of the old and some of the new, that which is unchanging and that which has been lovingly retouched.

Look carefully, in the book and in the town. The spirit survives. Some can be yours.

The original courthouse, built in 1881, **above**, has been restored through the generosity of a donor and is now the Public Library, one of the most creative adaptive-reuse buildings in Texas. The reconstructed Vereins Kirche (community church), **right**, originally built in 1847 in an octagonal fachwerk (framework) design, stands in the central square of town.

The kitchen of this limestone house built in the 1860's boasts a raised hearth fireplace for ease of cooking.

This kitchen combines the beauty of its rock walls with modern cooking facilities for the contemporary gourmet.

This unassuming frame house, **left**, is reminiscent of the simplicity and spareness so admired in Shaker design. Rough wood and stone walls, **above and right**, make stunning backgrounds for both old and new objects.

Antique crockery and utensils, this page, decorate these kitchens. Buildings, opposite, from another time, lovingly maintained and preserved.

A cheery red-and-black blanket and bold quilts enliven the bedroom of this log cabin built in 1846–47, the first winter of Fredericksburg's existence.

The logs of the early cabins were often numbered before construction began, making them Texas' first prefabricated homes.

A lone rock house, **left**, sits quietly in its bucolic setting. Log walls, **this page**, provide a striking background for the skillfully crafted Texas-German furniture eagerly sought by collectors today.

The owners' love of wood and authentic early furniture is evident throughout this home.

A magnificent four-poster bed with antique pillow shams and a yo-yo quilt are the focus of this bedroom.

The red-and-white theme picked up in the dress of the girl in the lithograph is repeated with linens and tulips. This bedroom was constructed of old materials to be compatible with the original structure—a schoolhouse built in the 1890's.

Each item has been carefully selected for its handmade quality by the artist who sleeps in this bedroom.

A cedar tree much like the early pioneers might have had graces this room with Christmas cheer.

Verbena, coreopsis, and rosemary share this country kitchen garden.

A tobacco-drying basket and rake, **above**, are given the white space often accorded fine pieces of sculpture. There is an inviting softness to this room, **right**. The unusual rock pattern, called Babel stonework, was intended to be plastered. When left exposed, it creates an interesting design element.

This cozy corner invites one to daydream by the open door.

An early portrait and bride's boxes from Germany surround this fireplace. The lovely hooked rug was made by a talented Fredericksburg craftswoman.

This one-story rock house, **left**, was built with practicality as well as beauty in mind. The back door and windows are aligned with the front, creating a cool, breeze-filled house in summer. A child's room, **above**, safe and secure for dreaming long nights' dreams.

*The bedroom, **left**, takes on an entirely new look when different colored quilts are used. This charming bedroom, **above**, has twin Button beds from the mid-1860's covered with blue-and-white quilts from the owner's collection. The two with the same design are called Bear Claw.*

One can envision a room complete in every detail, a replica from the late 1800's.

The newly crafted sleigh bed made of old pine by a local artisan is harmonious with objects that were handcrafted in another century.

A rusted farm implement, **opposite**, is etched against the dusk of a southwestern sky. Patterns are found everywhere, **this page**, even in the most ordinary places.

Collections of Santas, toy soldiers, and old family photographs bring pleasure to their owners. The stars were used as finials for the iron support rods in old Texas buildings.

Irises that brighten this white fence were divided and shared from the garden of a neighbor.

Details of this house include stenciling by the owner, who is self-taught.

There are visual surprises everywhere in this small Hill Country town.

Firkins, **left**, also called pantry boxes, are stacked up in a corner of the kitchen. Bride's boxes, **above**, were made in Germany and Pennsylvania and were meant to hold mementos from the wedding. Treasured for their floral decoration, they were passed down from generation to generation. This hallway, **opposite**, is made interesting by the owner's collections of checkerboards and blue-and-white stoneware.

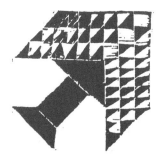

The kleiderschrank *(clothes cupboard) was one of the finest pieces built by the German cabinetmakers.*

The sun pierces a basket of wool, leaving the imprint of its weave on the wooden floor.

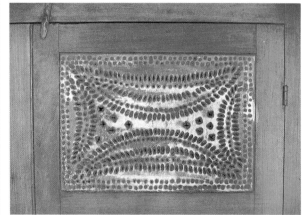

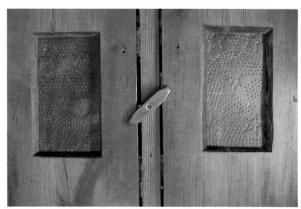

*Pie safes, **this page**, were decorated with punched tin panels to allow the air in and keep flies out. Stars and hearts were favorite motifs. The arrow design of this gate, **opposite**, was popular as fencing and can still be found throughout the town.*

*The quilt, **opposite**, lovingly handmade and often given as a gift, is used in a variety of ways to decorate old homes. Wood, **this page**, its paint mellowed and worn at points of contact, ages with a lustrous patina.*

This bathroom with its elegant chandelier and zinc-lined bathtub recalls the pleasure that must have accompanied the first indoor plumbing.

Some of the early paint colors were surprisingly bold and vibrant. The colors appear dull when exposed, only because they have faded and become dirty through the years.

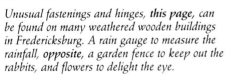

Unusual fastenings and hinges, **this page,** *can be found on many weathered wooden buildings in Fredericksburg. A rain gauge to measure the rainfall,* **opposite,** *a garden fence to keep out the rabbits, and flowers to delight the eye.*

The calm stillness outside, **this page,** is repeated by the grouping of objects inside. Rusted tin cans and license plates, **opposite,** have been recycled to shelter tender young plants from a late frost. Something of the practical pioneer spirit survives.

Almost everyone with a yard plants a garden. In the summer one can overhear conversations about the superiority of one variety of tomato over another.

"What is paradise? but a garden. . . ."—William Lawson, 1687

Living spaces for the birds as well.

*Scenes common to the town,
yet unique in character
because "old" is cherished.*

Calligraphy by M. L. Jeffreys
Woodcuts by Barbara Whitehead
Design by Whitehead & Whitehead